Once I *slice*, it relieves so much pressure I can *breathe*, again...

Help Me!

By: Donna M. Zadunajsky

Copyright

HELP ME! is a work of fiction. Names, characters, places, and incidents are either the product of the author's imagination or are used fictitiously. Any resemblance to actual persons, living or dead, events, or places is entirely coincidental or have been changed for the privacy of the living.

Dedication

This book goes out to my daughter and all her friends, and their friends, etc. So many kids and adults out there are suffering from something we all know as depression. There are so many that we don't always know who they are. They could be the person we sit next to on the bus or in our math class at school. They may not show any signs of self-destruction on the outside, but on the inside, they want to die, or at most, hurt themselves because they don't think they're good enough, pretty enough, or likable enough.

But the truth is, they are loved more than they know. Is it that they don't see it? Or is it that they don't *think* they're loveable enough for us? How is one person born without these thoughts and self-esteem issues, and another that just wants their world to end? Is it their lifestyle that makes them feel a certain way? Maybe a parent, an alcoholic or drug abuser is abusing them at home? We all live and are raised differently, but what makes us become so depressed that we want to end our life? I'm sure most of us have experienced some kind of bullying in our life. Maybe when we were in school, or maybe even at our job where we work. There's always someone who has to be better than us or get his or her own way. Maybe they feel more superior when they're bullying other people?

I don't know all the answers, but I do know that we need to do something about it.

Foreword

My editor suggested that I write a Foreword for this book to inform people of the growing epidemic facing our youth on the effects of bullying, including suicide. The only thing I know to do is to write from my heart, especially on the things I know about. I did not want this Novella to be a summary of a police suicide report or a recap of a Medical Examiner's findings.

When I first thought about writing this fictional book based upon a kid that my daughter knows, I was hesitant about it. To be candid, this book is also inspired by my own story. There have been moments when I, myself, felt the same way, but had never acted upon it. God forbid, I actually talked about what I was considering back when I was a teenager.

This Novella might hit home for many people. It might seem like I just wrote about their life. Truth is—it was written about someone's life, though names and some circumstances have been changed or modified to protect their identity. It is based on my daughter's best friend and the battle he faced and still deals with every day.

Is there more we can do for people like Mick? Can we listen a little more, or a little longer? Give them a hug or even sit and talk to them, with them? Can we protect them from what the world hands us?

I'm not sure how to answer these questions. But I do know that there were a couple of times in my life when I didn't want to face another day. I didn't want to live one more moment. This may surprise some people, but why write a book about a boy being depressed if I haven't myself felt some of the things Mick has felt?

I deal with days that I have to *will* myself to get through. I'm not sure what causes these downfalls, but I make it through them and the next thing I know, it's been days or weeks that have gone by and I feel great, but I also know that these thoughts will never completely go away. I can't explain the feelings that stir inside me, just as you probably can't explain what is going on inside yourself. Each person is different and we all deal with situations in our own way. Granted there are more programs and facilities out there now that can help people like us. Now it's just up to us to reach out and ask for HELP!

I did some research on local nonprofit organizations and websites that can help those of us who are thinking about ending our lives, or even self-injuring, such as what Mick was doing in this book. These websites have lists of hotlines for each state that include a free-bullying guide and suicide support groups where you can go and talk with people who are just like you and are going through something similar or as self-destructive. You're not the only one who might feel alone and is being bullied.

I honestly can't say that I wasn't surprised on how many different sites there are out there with just a click of a button. Something I didn't have back in the eighties when I was dealing with my depression and bullying. I didn't talk to anyone about what and how I was feeling; I just thought, I guess, it would be a better world without me in it.

Today, I'm more verbal about what I went through and what I felt. But, it was my daughter who brought that out of me because of her friends and what they are doing to themselves. I have several more books in this series to write. More stories to share about other teenage suicides happening each and every day. Although I don't know the whole story about what they're going through, I'm pretty sure I won't be too far off from the truth after writing it.

If you or someone you know needs guidance with what they're feeling or going through, and you don't want to talk to an adult in your household or an adult at your school, then I suggest turning to these websites for help. They are very resourceful and are there to help you understand and cope with depression and suicidal thoughts.

http://www.suicide.org
http://www.helpguide.org
http://www.selfinjury.com.

You can also call the numbers listed here when you're ready to get help, 1-800-SUICIDE or 1-800-273-TALK.

There are so many untold stories out there. So many that need told. I just want you to know that you're not alone, and that there are people out there that will listen and can help you. I'm not a medical doctor or professional counselor, but I'm here if you need someone to just listen to whatever you need to talk about at dmzadunajsky@gmail.com Just reach out and ask for help. I'm also available to schools or other organizations for speaking out about suicide and bullying.

Help Me!

Part One

Mick's Story

Mick

I think it's best that I start by introducing myself. Will it be important? I guess I'll leave that up to you in the end. I think introductions are the best so if I tell you who I am, then you'll at least know something about me, but then by the end of my story you'll know all about me. You'll know why I do what I do. Why I'm going to do what needs to be done. Should have been done...

My name is Mick, Mick Connors. I live in the south suburbs of Chicago. I'm thirteen years old, and I have two half siblings, a brother and a sister. I don't see them much, but in all reality, I don't care. They live with my mom a couple of towns away. I'm supposed to go to my mom's house every other weekend, but my dad lets me stay home. He doesn't force me to see her. She's the reason why they're not together anymore. It's one of the reasons why I live with my dad and not her! Well, if you haven't figured it out yet, I have given you two clues... Yep, that's right, the half siblings.

Their divorce caught me unexpectedly. I mean... they seemed so together. Like they knew what they were doing, but then—*Wham!* It was like I was sucker-punched in the gut when they broke the news to me.

Okay, so if I look back and think about some of their fights, yeah, I can see that they had their moments, but divorce? That's like—final. There's no, "I'm just kidding", or "We can always just rip up the papers and act like it never happened." No, divorce is divorce. It means it's over and there's no going back. We tried, but I can't stand living with you anymore, so yeah, goodbye.

Seven months later, after my dad moved out, she was getting ready to give birth to my half brother and sister. I'm not sure what surprised me more—the divorce or the fact she cheated on my dad and got herself pregnant. I don't even want to think about it anymore.

* * * * *

I hate everything about school. I hate getting up in the morning to go. I hate the classes they make me take. I hate all the teachers. I don't think I've ever liked any of my teachers in all the time I've been in school. But mostly, I hate the kids that go to the school. Well, at least the ones that are mean to me. The ones that bully me!

So now you know my parents are divorced and I live with my dad. You know I have two half siblings and that I hate school.

One more thing, I used to live with my mom, but since the start of eighth grade, I've been living with my dad. They say it's for the best, you know, because of what happened to my best friend. Oh, I guess I haven't told you that part yet...

Accident

It's been four months since the accident. "Accident," I whisper, as if that were what it really was. Four months since my friend was found dead in his bedroom. I'll have to take the story back before the accident so that way you'll get the *jiffs* of what really happened to my best friend.

My best friend's name was Ray, Ray Mullion. He was younger than me by three months, but at the time, he was the same age as me. I'm not sure if that's significant or not.

He lived a couple of houses down from me. We met in first grade when he moved here from Iowa. He stood by me through everything since we were six. I wish I'd been a better friend to him as he was to me, back then. Maybe, just maybe, he'd still be alive.

Where my mom lives in Stuart, Illinois, is where we lived growing up, but now I live with my dad in Homer, Illinois, which is in Will County. Like I said at the beginning, I moved here after the accident.

With all the technology these days, there's a lot of cyber-bullying going on. So much that parents don't know what to do about it. I'm sure most parents don't even know what their child is doing when they're on their cell phone or computer. What they're posting or even saying to other kids. Or in some cases, what other kids are saying and doing to them.

Here's an example of one of the texts I kept from my friend Ray's Snap/Chat account. It was a hate account set-up for him by someone we didn't know or maybe we did and we just never figured it out yet.

From unknown person:

trill.em.ray.hate.account

Seriously, this faggot needs to get a f***ing life and get some real friends and stop f***ing posting depressing shit! If he hates his life, he should f***ing kill himself and make us all happy!

Ray responded:

trill.em.ray

Who is this?

From unknown person:

trill.em.ray.hate.account

Go hang yourself!

HELP ME!

Ray responded:

trill.em.ray

Who tf is this? OMFG!

From unknown person:

trill.em.ray.hate.account

You are a waste of f***ing oxygen!

It took Ray an hour on the computer before he was able to hack into the account and take it over. I still don't know who did it, or why? That was the start of his depression.
At first, I thought he was joking about killing himself, but I guess in the end, the jokes on me. If I'd taken him seriously, then maybe he'd still be here. Then maybe, I'd take my life more seriously and not think about suicide myself...

Suicide

Did you know that nearly thirty thousand people commit suicide every year? That suicide is the third leading cause of death for fifteen to twenty-four-year-olds and second leading for twenty-four to thirty-five-years-olds? They say on average, one person commits suicide every seventeen minutes. How about this: A one in sixty-five thousand children ages ten to fourteen commit suicide each year!

I guess you can say I've done my research, but it still doesn't take away the thoughts of suicide from my mind.

Have you ever had one of those days where everything comes crashing down at once? Everything bad just comes out of nowhere and eats at you? That's how I've been feeling ever since my friend Ray took his own life.

He didn't take pills to make himself fall asleep, poison himself, or hang himself by asphyxiation. No! Ray chose to take his dad's .44 Special and blow his f***ing brains out! I overheard the cops say that there was only one bullet in the gun, as if he played Russian roulette by himself and lost.

It was actually a game we'd played a couple of times together. You know, like a dare, but nothing had ever happened, of course.

Sometimes I feel so angry inside and want to destroy everything in my sight. A part of me even feels responsible for my friend dying. Like, I could've stopped him from doing it.

* * * * *

I knew my friend Ray was being bullied. In fact, we both were, by the same kids at my old school. Neither one of us said anything to the teachers or principal that we were being bullied. Nothing will ever be done to them, and in all reality, does it even matter? Ray's dead. He's never coming back, and they're responsible for it.

Ray kept getting hate email from some unknown accounts. They call it cyber-bullying, but nothing ever seems to be done about it. Kids will continue doing it no matter what. There's no stopping them from being mean to other people.

The week and days before his death, Ray became more distant towards me. He shut me out of his life. Like he didn't need me or want me around him. That right there should've told me something. No, I think the day before gave me a definite clue and yet, I didn't do anything. I didn't say anything to anyone.

The last time I saw Ray was the same night he killed himself. I went to his house after school. He actually begged me to hang out with him just like old times. We were in his room, messing around when he went to the nightstand beside his bed and pulled out the gun. My eyes drew wide; I think I was more in shock than anything. Though we'd played that game I'd told you about, but I didn't think he kept the gun in his room. Kept it beside him while he slept. That's when he asked me if I ever thought about death.

"Hey Mick, have you ever thought about ending your life so you don't have to put up with those assholes from school anymore?" Ray had asked.

I shrugged, "Sometimes, I guess." What really could I say? It made me nervous, watching him hold the gun.

The gun was in one palm, and he kept flipping it over and back again. It was as if he wanted to look at both sides at the same time. He stared at it as if he was transfixed in some way. After several minutes, he placed the gun back in the nightstand as if it were an everyday routine.
Couple of hours later, I walked home. It was the last time I saw him alive. The gun went off at exactly midnight. How do I know that? Because it was the exact same time I sat up in bed, knowing something bad had just happened. Something I'll live the rest of my life trying to forget. Wondering if I could have saved him...

Bullying

I will always remember what happened four months ago. I don't think I'll ever feel like me again. Feel happy and carefree. Instead, I hate myself for letting my friend die. It's why I do what I do.

I flip the razor blade between my fingers; just one slice will make the thoughts disappear, at least for today. I started cutting a week after my friend's funeral. It's a way for me to release the pain I feel inside, you know, for not saving him.

The same kids at school, after what happened, continued to bully me. They didn't care that Ray was dead; in fact, they insisted that I do the same because I was worthless and unneeded in this world. That their life would be so much better without me in it.

When the school year ended two months later, that's when I came to live with my dad. My parents thought it would be best if I started over some place new. They don't know about the bullying, or that I cut.

Most of the time, I sit in my bedroom, away from other people. My dad works Monday through Friday from ten in the morning until nine at night. So my days consist of sitting in my room searching the web and making new cuts on my forearm when I start to feel depressed and all alone.

I wear long sleeves so no one can see the marks, and sometimes I make cuts on the inside of my leg. I barely eat, mostly because I was teased at my old school about being overweight, so now I just nibble on food, here and there. Like I said, my dad works all the time, so it's not like he watches me. The less conversation we have the better, as far as I'm concerned.

* * * * *

Since the start of eighth grade, there's this one girl, Layla Manning, who steals the very breath I breathe. Every morning when I get off the bus, I look for her before she heads off to her Chorus class. I feel like it's something I have to do before I head inside to go to my first period class.

We have no classes together, which sucks, but when I have time, I hurry to where her locker is so I can see her pretty face, see that gorgeous smile she gives me when I walk slowly by her.

I'm not the best looking guy in the school, which is why it surprises me that she always smiles at me. It took me until the middle of the school year to get the nerve to talk to her.

She's friends with a kid who is, or who I want to be, my best friend, but I'm not sure I want to have that attachment with someone again. To get so close and then something bad happens to them.

HELP ME!

So like I was saying, she's a friend of Shawn Bowers. He's a really cool kid, and we have this connection that is sort of hard to explain. He is the only boy in eighth grade that has a mustache, though I think he's a year older than me because I heard he failed first grade. His hair is black and curly, unlike mine that is dark brown and straight. I mousse the front of my hair so it sticks up, but in a messy way.

So, back to Shawn. He's a little shorter than my six-foot two inches, but he has this bad-ass way about him. I've noticed he's always getting into trouble. I swear I see him sitting in detention every day for either not doing his homework or talking back to the teacher. I just shake my head because I know he doesn't care about getting into trouble. I wish I were more like him. Then maybe I'd stand up for myself and not get bullied by the other kids.

Now a little about this girl Layla. She's thirteen years old and her birthday is in May. She has long straight brown hair that lies down her entire back. I like to get as close to her as possible because her hair smells like grapes; it's intoxicating. Her teeth are straight from the braces she recently had removed, and her smile is sweet and pushes her cheeks up just right so that one single dimple appears in her left cheek. She always has a lot of friends hanging around her. Yeah, I would say she's in the popular group.

None of my friends at Homer know about the cuts on my arms and legs. Though, neither do my parents, so I guess no one knows what I do when I'm alone...

Social Media

I'm Sorry

Sometimes, I get jealous thinking that

someone else could make you happier than I could.

I guess it's my insecurities acting up.

Because I know I'm not the prettiest, smartest, or most fun and exciting.

But, I do know that no matter how hard and

long you look; you'll never

find somebody that loves you like I do…

—Anonymous

I have a Snap/Chat and Instagram account that I post things on, just like all the other kids at my school. It's how I express what I'm feeling without actually coming out and telling anyone. The quote I just wrote is how I feel when I'm around Layla. She makes the world I live in, worth living. I know I shouldn't give one person all that I have left of myself, but with her, I can't help feeling the way I do. I can't help loving her with all my heart...

I guess in all reality that's not right of me to do, but I just can't help it around her. She's amazing, pretty, smart, and she talks to me. We chat on Kik, and lately, we've been FaceTiming with one another. I love hearing her sweet voice and seeing her face. She says I'm one of her best friends. Sometimes, a few of us, Layla, CJ, Shawn, Tyler, who I think is her boyfriend, and I go on Oovoo, which is sort of like FaceTime, but you can have up to twelve people at once to talk to, but you can only see four. It's pretty cool.

Sometimes, Layla's mom says "hi" to everyone. She comes into Layla's room, a lot, which isn't a bad thing, but sometimes I just want to be alone with Layla. Talking and being around her makes me not want to cut myself.

* * * * *

I'm back to cutting myself. Not cutting, only lasted a week, because I started thinking about and remembering the people who treat me like crap. I hate them all, but at the same time if they were to ask me for a favor, I would do it because I'm too kind-hearted.

I think I have a major depression disorder. When I have a big downward swing that lasts, I feel like the easiest way to bring myself out of it, is by showing myself exactly how much I'm putting myself through. I also know that physical pain releases chemicals in the brain that will make me feel better, even if only for a short time. I can take the physical pain over emotional pain, any time.

I cut because I hate myself, sometimes. I feel like a malfunctioning machine that just can't do what it's supposed to do. I rarely get urges to cause anyone else any type of pain, but I have no problem slicing my own arm with a razor.

In fact, I have always been happiest when I am comforting someone else. I don't know why. I'm overcome with a sense of loneliness. I feel there's me in one corner, and the entire planet in another. I have never felt like I belonged anywhere.

I cut when the sadness is coupled with a rage that I can't even put into words. Rage that no one ever hears me. I only cut when I'm feeling down on myself that I can think of no other way to handle matters. I want to die so badly, but I just don't have the guts to off myself.

Since Ray, cutting is my best friend. It takes away the emotional pain, when I can barely breathe from all the pain I feel inside from losing him. When I'm too anxious and I can't handle life, it's like a tranquilizer that prevents me from a panic attack. Best of all it gives me an alternative to suicide...

Sorry

I wish I wouldn't let myself be so attached to someone. I wish I didn't love so easy, especially when it comes to a girl like Layla. I guess I expected her to love me back. To always be there when I needed her. She doesn't know what I do to my body. She can never know what I do. I'm certain, she'd never be my friend again. She'll think I'm a freak and not want to talk to me anymore. I don't think I could handle her not being in my life. Although I'd love to have her as my girlfriend, I will forever love her as my friend, if that's all I can have.

I've been posting on my Instagram how I feel lately. This quote I found explains everything:

I'm sorry I constantly want to talk to you.
I'm sorry when you take long to reply, I get sad.
I'm sorry if I say things that might piss you off.
I'm sorry if I come off as annoying.
I'm sorry if you don't want to talk to me
as much as I wanna talk to you.

HELP ME!

I'm sorry if I think about you too much

and too often.

I'm sorry if I tell you about my pointless drama when you don't really care.

I'm sorry if I come off as being clingy, but it's just me missing you…

—Anonymous

* * * * *

I miss Layla not talking to me. I'm not even sure what I said that pissed her off to the point she won't even text me. I can't go on without her talking to me. I can't stand it; not hearing her voice, or reading her texts.

I need to cut to make the emotional pain go away. I reach beside my bed, pull out the iPod case inside my nightstand drawer, and open it. The razor blade stares up at me, calling out to me. I grab it and place the box on the bed. With the razor between my fingers, I press the blade against my skin and slowly cut through all three layers of skin. I watch the skin separate. I suck in a breath, hold it as the blood beads around the cut, and then it slides down my arm. It feels so good.

Once I exhale, all is right in my world again…

Layla

Winter break has arrived, which gives me more time to sit around and think about why I'm still alive and why Layla doesn't want to talk to me anymore. I miss her...

I wrote her a letter, but there's no way of giving it to her. We don't live that close together. Actually, I'm not sure where she lives, exactly.

My iPod starts ringing; I look down and see who wants to Face Time with me.

It's her.

It's my Layla.

She's actually calling me. My hands start to shake, and I wonder why it's taking me so long to answer the call. I breathe in deep, and tap the icon.

"Hi," Layla says.

"Hi," I say back.

"How's your winter break going?" she asks.

"Good, I guess."

"Cool," she replies, and then is quiet.

I can see part of her face and wonder what she's thinking about. I wonder if it's me she's thinking of. Maybe that's why she called. Maybe she misses me too.

I decide to ask her what she's been doing since school let out. "How's your break going?"

"It's alright, bored as all hell."

"Ya', me too. My dad's at work so I can't really go anywhere, and it's too cold to go outside."

"That's sucks," she agrees. "I'm just lying in bed, watching TV. I don't feel like doing much today."

We both get quiet, letting the silence fill the words we aren't speaking. I don't know why I'm going to tell her what I'm about to say. Maybe to see her reaction. "I wrote you a letter," I say and swallow, praying she doesn't get mad at me, again.

"You wrote me a letter? When can I read it?" she says, smiling.

"I guess when we go back to school," I reply.

"That's like two weeks away! I can't wait that long," she shrieks. "Can't you bring it to my house?"

I never thought about doing that, though that was before she called me. "I'll have to call my dad and ask. Will your mom be able to come and get me?" I ask with my fingers crossed.

"I'll ask my mom and then you can ask your dad."

"Okay," I reply. I can see her get out of bed and walk through the room. I hear silence; which means she must have muted her end to talk to her mom.

Minutes go by before she returns and says "Yes," I can come over and that her mom will come and pick me up. I hang up with her and call my dad to ask if it'd be okay if I went to Layla's house and that her mom can pick me up and drop me off later. He says I can, but I'll need to be home by eight, which is five hours away. I can't believe I'm going over to Layla's house. I quickly text her back that I can and go get ready. She replies it'll be about an hour.

Perfect!

* * * * *

I keep looking out the window for her to arrive. I'm so excited I can't control my happiness. I see a car coming down the road, and then it turns around. A text comes through from Layla asking if I could stand outside so they can find the right house. The same car that I saw moments ago pulls in front of the house.

The window goes down and I see Layla in the backseat. I run around the car and climb in. Layla's mom introduces herself before driving away.

In the front seat, I see that Layla's friend Allie is with us. I'm a little disappointed, but I'm with Layla and that's all that matters.

Layla must have seen the disappointment on my face because at that moment, she sends me a text that she can't have any boys at the house without another girl present. I text back, "That's okay."

Even though I'm disappointed that Allie is with us, I'm just glad it's not Bailey. She's one of Layla's friends that I *really* can't stand. She stirs up so much drama and makes such a big deal out of everything.

I. Can't. Stand. Her.

She's one of the reasons why I feel I need to cut. She's such a bitch!

The car ride only lasts ten minutes, when we pull into a drive with a gate and then drive through, turning into another driveway to the right. This huge house appears, and then we're backing into the garage. Once inside the house, Layla takes us into her bedroom, and then shows me the rest of the house before going downstairs.

The downstairs is the same length as the floor upstairs. Layla and Allie walk around a bar to an area where there are three cushioned chairs. I pass an air hockey machine on my way to the chairs. Behind the chairs, there's a pool table. She tells me her parents love Elvis and The Beatles, which I sort of figured out on my own. All the walls surrounding me have nothing but Elvis and The Beatles on them. Though, there was this one wall that had pictures of her parents with several different movie stars like Robin Williams and Robert England, just to name a few.

Layla grabs a remote from the counter and the next thing I know, a screen lowers from the ceiling. She asks if there's anything I'd like to watch. I shake my head. I honestly don't care what we do as long as I'm with her.

* * * * *

Next thing I know, it's time for me to leave. Although part of me wishes Allie wasn't here, I still had a great time hanging out with Layla. In the car back to my house, I slide her the letter I wrote and then get out of the car...

Alone

Things are different now, we're drifting apart,
and I don't know how to fix it.
You're starting to become closer to other people,
and I'm just sitting here watching the
world go by without me. I don't know what to do, it hurts.
I hope this is just a phase and we will get over it
because if not I won't know what to do…

—Anonymous

I'm not sure why, but I don't sleep like most people. My mind is always racing, and I find myself staying up until three or four in the morning. I kind of know why I can't sleep. Ever since my friend's death, I can't seem to close my eyes without seeing him. Seeing him put the gun in his mouth and actually pulling the trigger. I wasn't there when it happened as you know, but the images seem and feel so real, as if I were…

I went four days without cutting, since my time with Layla. Everything was fine, and then *bam* I'm back to loneliness and self-destruction. I'm not sure, but I think when I was at her house, she might have seen the cuts on my forearm that I usually cover with my jacket, but sometimes I forget and push my sleeves up too far and don't even realize that I'm doing it. She seems different, like she's afraid of me now. I don't know if I can handle her not wanting to be my friend.

I know I mentioned this earlier, but I just can't see my life without Layla in it. I don't think I can handle living without her. We're not boyfriend and girlfriend, but I'd like us to be. That's probably like putting myself out on the ledge and actually jumping to my death.

I don't know what she thought about the letter I had written. Since her place, she hasn't video chatted with me. My mind starts to whirl and I think of more things that are negative. *What if* Layla doesn't talk to me again? *What if* everyone at school finds out about the cuts, and I'm laughed at, or worse, told to kill myself like the kids at my last school? Maybe that's why Ray did what he did. Maybe he decided to accept the dare and just do it. End everything!

I pull the small box from the side of my bed and open it. The one thing that holds my life in its hands—my razor blade. I pick it up and set the empty box down on my bed in front of me. I push the sleeve of my sweatshirt up, revealing the crevice of my forearm and elbow. The cuts I made last week are scabbed over. I have scars from the cuts prior to the recent ones I've made. Ten in a row on one arm and fifteen or more on the other. I haven't even counted the ones on the inside of my thighs.

Some are small cuts, maybe a quarter to half an inch. The others I would say are an inch or so longer.

The books I've read about suicide said that if you're going to kill yourself by cutting your wrist, it's best to cut along the length of your arm.

* * * * *

It's eight o'clock on a Friday night, and my iPod starts to ring. It's Layla calling. I hit the Oovoo icon and instantly we're connected. She's smiling at me, but she can't see my face because I have the camera facing the ceiling.

"Hi," she says.

"Hey," I reply.

"I read your letter and decided to write you one back, but I'll just give it to you on Monday when we go back to school," Layla states.

I'm smiling, but I don't let her see me. Maybe I was wrong and she hadn't seen my scars, my cuts. I'm still holding the blade that I just used to cut into my arm. The blood makes a run down the side of my arm, and then Layla's voice brings me back to the present. I grab a Kleenex from the nightstand and place it on the cut. Without realizing, I say "ouch" and I can see Layla's eyes widen a little. She looks curious, as if she knows what I've just done.

I hear her mom come into the room, and then she says hello to me. "Hi, Mom," I say back to her. Most of the kids Layla talks to, call her "Mom" or Mrs. Manning. I prefer to call her mom, as she's nicer than my own mom. If you knew my mom, then you'd say the same thing.

I get my stash of gauze and place it on the cut, taping it down on my arm, and pull my sleeve over it. I hear Layla's mom ask where I was so I make my face visible.

Layla and I talk for several hours, until she falls asleep, and we're eventually disconnected...

Cut

Monday arrives before I know it. I didn't fall asleep until three and I'm barely awake to go to school, but my dad makes sure I'm up and ready for the bus to come in fifteen minutes.

Once on the bus, I place the earbuds in my ears and tune out all the kids around me. Music fills my ears, and I'm suddenly taken away to another place in my mind. A place I'd rather be than where I have to be. I'm not sure that makes sense to you, but it doesn't have to.

The bus pulls into the the school and from my seat I can see Layla and her friend Allie walking to the middle school, which is across the parking lot from Homer Jr. High, and where Chorus is taught. Shawn tags along behind them, and I can see her laughing at something he said. I wish I was with them.

* * * * *

The best part about lunch is that I get to share it with Shawn. I don't eat lunch; I just sit there and talk and joke around. Shawn doesn't know how I feel about Layla so I guess I shouldn't be surprised when he tells me that he likes her more than a friend.

"Do you think if I ask her to be my girlfriend, she will?" Shawn asks.

I shrug my shoulders. Now that Layla and Tyler broke up, Shawn thinks he can date her or, at least, wants to date her. Not wanting him to know that she's mine, though she isn't mine, I just don't want to share her, though she isn't mine to share. "How does she act when you're around?" I ask.

"She's always laughing at my jokes," he exclaims. "But if I ask her and she says no, I don't want us not to be friends. I don't want her to feel awkward around me."

"Well," I start to say. "You'll have to figure out a way to ask and let her know that you don't want to lose her as a friend." I paste a smile on my face, praying she'll say no to him.

"Yeah, I'll think about it first before saying anything to her," Shawn replies, then goes back to eating his lunch.

I nod, and then stare-off in another direction, thinking of only one thing... one person...

* * * * *

I was hoping that when I came to this school that I wouldn't be bullied again. That the kids at this school were better people than at my old school. I couldn't have been more wrong!

Ayman Raheem is one of the biggest assholes I know, and he's one of the meanest bullies I've come across in all my years in school—period! He has nothing nice to say to anyone, especially me. He makes fun of the way I style my hair, the way I talk, and the way I walk. He's such an ass...

He gets off making fun of other kids and belittling them. I want to kick his ass so much, but I'm not a fighter. I know I can fight. I know that if I allow all the anger I have in my body to build, I will burst. I could hurt someone; possibly send them to the hospital needing stitches. Maybe that's who I am now. Maybe I'm an angry person who wants to get revenge for my best friend killing himself.

In the gym locker room, Ayman pushes me up against the lockers and calls me a f***ing faggot and that I'd better stay away from him, unless I want to get my ass kicked. I mumble that I'm not a faggot, and he says, "Well, you look like a faggot, you f***ing fag." Everyone in the room laughs at me, and then bolts when they hear the coach shout from the open door that we have two minutes to get finished and get in the gym.

* * * * *

I arrive at my house at two-thirty and text my dad that I'm home from school. The first thing I do is go into my bedroom and grab the box that holds the most precious thing in my life.

My razor blade.

I open the box and grab the sharp blade.

I toss the box on the bed and push up the shirt-sleeve on my arm, showing my cuts.

I press the tip of the blade into my skin and slice a two-inch cut across my forearm.

Within seconds, blood appears; I feel the release of today's worries, and all the evil thoughts disappear...

Gun

The first Friday in February arrives, and the same weekend of the Super Bowl. I'm looking forward to getting out of school for a couple of days. I can't stand the feeling I have inside. I want to cut so badly, but I can't, I have to leave my razor at home. I can't take the chance of having the school find out about what I do and how I feel about life.

* * * * *

At lunch today, Shawn tells me Layla said she just wants to be friends with him. She's not interested in dating right now. At least, he had the nerve to ask her out.

I look at the clock on the wall, "When the hell is the bell going to ring," I mumble under my breath. Just as I say the words, the bell rings abrupt and loud, making me jump straight out of my chair.

I head to my locker and toss my books inside. Just like every day, I do all my homework in school so I don't have to do any of it at home. I'm not sure if that's good or bad. It gives me more time to think about my life. About Layla.

Allie, who is Layla's friend, asked me out yesterday, but I haven't given her an answer. It's not her I want. I guess I'll have to give it more thought; maybe I should move on with someone else, but I know my heart won't be in it.

I do my usual as I step off the steps of the bus and make my way to the front door of my house. The minute I tap into our Wi-Fi, I text my dad that I'm home from school. I shut the front door behind me and open the refrigerator. Like every day, I grab a coke and head straight to my bedroom. I plop down on my bed and lean back against the headbroad.

Most of the time when I'm alone, I search for quotes that express how I feel at that moment or how I've felt all day.

I think about death a lot, like I think we all do.

I don't think of suicide as an option, but as fun.

It's an interesting idea that you can control how you go.

It's this thing that's looming, and you can control it.

~ ~

We can consciously end our life almost anytime we choose.

This ability is an endowment, like laughing and

blushing, given to no other animal...

in any given moment, by not exercising

the option of suicide, we are choosing to live.

—*Anonymous*

This last quote makes me think and analyze the past few years of my life. All the bullying I had endured at my last school, and now here. I can't believe all the hateful things kids and people can say to each other. Like they don't care how it makes others feel. Making us feel less alive and less human than others. Like some of us shouldn't be here and others should. Who gave them the right to treat us differently? Like they are better than everyone else!

* * * * *

I stand and open the door to my room. I cross the hall and go into my dad's bedroom. I know right where he hides his handgun. I open the closet and reach up for the box he has hidden on the top shelf, then go back to my room. I sit Indian style on the floor and remove the lid from the box in front of me. My dad's Ruger SP101 revolver stares back at me.

Images of my friend Ray flash through my mind—wondering if he thought the same thoughts I'm thinking in this particular moment. Did he know what he was doing? Did he realize there were no take-backs once the trigger is pulled?

I take the gun from the box and hold it in my hand. My finger rests on the trigger, though I know there aren't any bullets in the gun. My dad doesn't keep it loaded, but the bullets are in the box with the gun. I push the button and the cylinder opens on the side. I place one bullet in and close it.

I spin the gun on the wood floor of my bedroom. Sometimes, just to see what it feels like, I place the tip of the gun against my temple, but I have never once pulled the trigger. No!

I'm more into the slice the blade makes against my skin and the blood running down my arm.

It relieves so much pressure. I can breathe again...

Thoughts

Layla calls me right after I hide the gun in the nightstand next to my bed. I'll just keep it here for a few days, before putting it back in my dad's closet. I hope that he doesn't go looking for it. That would be really bad.

Layla and I talk for an hour, and then she's called to have dinner. She says she'll call me later. I spend my time searching the web and flicking through the channels on the TV. Nothing ever seems to be on, at least anything that interests me, but I'm just passing time.

I must have fallen asleep, which is rare for me to do, because the sound of my iPod ringing startles me. I rub the sleep from my eyes, and then look for my iPod. It goes silent because I wasn't quick enough to answer it. Layla's name appears. Two missed calls. Before I'm able to call her, she starts calling me back.

"Hey," I say, before she has a chance to talk first.

"Hi," she replies. "Was worried for a minute."

"Worried about what?" I ask.

"I read the quotes you posted on Kik and Snap/Chat. Is everything okay with you? Do you want to talk about anything? I hope you know that you're my best friend and that you can talk to me about anything," Layla says, looking worried.

I can hear the concern in her voice, but I can't tell her that I cut. *But,* I already know she knows. My mind starts to whirl and I feel a panic attack coming on. I feel the urge to grab my razor and cut. Before I can stop myself, I end the call and grab the box beside my bed. She tries calling me back, but I refuse to answer. I can't talk to her, knowing she knows what I do. She'll try to change my mind. Try to get me to stop cutting. She won't understand why I have to do it!

I send her a text that I can't talk right now. She texts back, okay, but to text her so she knows that I'm okay. Once again, she says that I can talk to her anytime about anything.

I don't text her back...

Last Breath

Saturday crawls by, probably because I just sit in my room doing nothing. I don't feel like hanging out with my dad, though I know I should, just so he doesn't think there's something going on and starts getting into my business. I don't need him knowing what I put myself through. It's not his problem anyway. Yeah, sure, I'm only fourteen f***ing years old, but that don't give him a reason to know everything I do and who I hang out with.

I know. I know. What's with the f***ing attitude today? I guess I'm just tired of living. Tired of going to school with the same assholes every day. The same bullies that don't have anything better to do but belittle and downgrade everyone else whenever they want to.

Life just f***ing sucks!

I hate life!

I hate my f***ing life!

I just want it all to stop. I want it all to end!

But, there's only one way to do that, and that's the Ray way. Now I know why he did what he did.

* * * * *

It's Super Bowl Sunday. My dad's in the other room watching the game, and I'm in my room Oovooing with Layla, Tyler, and Shawn. One of them wants Bailey to connect, but I said no. Layla knows how I feel about her, and she texts me to just ignore her. So I do.

We each have the game on at our houses, as we Oovoo one another. Layla's mom checks in every now and then and says "hello" to everyone. She's rooting for the New England Patriots, who are playing the Seattle Seahawks. Layla's mom does this checking in with Layla every commercial break. She's funny like that sometimes.

During the game, the weather outside gets worse. The school's automated service calls everyone's house and cancels school for tomorrow. We are all happy and cheering.

An hour later, the game is over and the New England Patriots win by four. Tyler says goodbye, and Bailey, thank God, left a while ago. Now it's just Shawn, Layla, and me. We're all sort of doing our own thing. Layla is watching something on TV. Shawn has his earbuds in doing something on his iPad, or whatever he has in his hands. But me, I have my dad's Ruger SP101 revolver in my hand, while my iPod is facing the ceiling on mute.

I've been sitting on the floor on the other side of my bed, just in case my dad decides to pop his head in. That way I'll have time to hide the gun.

He usually just goes right to bed without saying a word, but then there's that off-chance he'll say goodnight. He's always in bed around ten every night. Grown-ups, they just can't stay up all night like we can. If you want to count the hours of sleep I've had since last Thursday that would be about six hours total.

My body's feeling it today too, but I just won't let my eyes shut. I open the cylinder and place one bullet in the gun. I spin it and close it quick. I place the tip of the revolver in my mouth and pull the trigger. I didn't even hesitate when I did it. I knew I had eight chances to get it right, and that was my first.

I spin the cylinder again, and place it back in my mouth.

Click.

That's two.

This time before pulling the trigger, I don't even bother spinning the cylinder. Besides, what's the use if I want to end my life tonight, I should just continue until it's done and I'm lying dead on my bedroom floor and all those asshole bullies at school can kiss my white ass because then I've won. I will no longer have to put up with their f***ing mouths ever again...

Click.

That's three.

Before I try again, I get a text from Layla. "What are you doing?" That's when I notice my iPod is facing me and that she probably saw everything. I send a text that I'll see her around sometime, but also that I won't be in school on Tuesday, and end my call on Oovoo.

I close my eyes, place the tip of the gun back in my mouth, and pull the trigger...

Part Two

Layla's Story

Layla

Hi, my name is Layla Ann Manning. I live in Homer, Illinois, and I go to Homer Jr. High. My mom and I moved here when I was eight from Naples, Florida. I don't remember much of my life in Florida, just that my real dad lives there with his new wife and kids. I don't remember much of him either.

Life in Illinois has been good to me so far. Although there are some moments when I want to move back down to Florida so I can be with my best friend Lynn. Lynn and I met when we were four years old at the pool near one of the places we lived. My dad took me there when my mom had to clean someone's house.

My mom and new dad, who adopted me, go down to Florida once a year during spring break. When I'm down there, I mostly hang out with my old classmate Mike, and of course, my best friend Lynn. Before I know it, it's time to leave, but I don't want to leave and come back to Chicago. Once I get home, I'm glad to be back with my friends again. I know, weird, right?

Besides texting with my friends, Face Time, Oovoo, and Kik, and now Snap/Chat. I'm either downstairs doing flips in the basement or at tumbling, which is only on Thursdays.

I used to take dance, but after a year of Jazz, I told my mom that I didn't want to do it anymore. Although mostly, it was because I didn't want to perform in front of all those people—I get nervous.

I thought about singing, but again, I would be on stage in front of all those people. I wish I knew how Taylor Swift does it all the time. God, to be like her, famous and beautiful. I love that she writes her own songs. I write my own quotes. I have a book of them, and I even save them in a folder in my email account.

Random Quotes by Layla Manning

* I have so many daydreams every day, and you are by far, the best one I have ever had.

* Love is painful and beautiful.

* I'm not trying to be perfect; it's not like it's worth it; besides everyone hurts the same.

* Let them miss you. Sometimes when you're available, they take you for granted because they think you'll always stay...

School

Since the start of eighth grade, I have most of the same friends from third grade when I moved here from Florida. Some, I don't talk to because they're in different classes than I am now, or we just grew apart.

There is one friend that my parents can't stand; her name is Bailey. They say there's just something about her they just don't like. I don't see what they're talking about; I think she's pretty fun to hang out with.

However, my mom allows her to spend just about every weekend at our house. She says I need to widen my horizon and have different friends sleep over. "Make new friends", she says. The thing is, most or all of my friends are boys, and I don't think they'd be allowed over, especially to spend the night.

Shawn is my newest friend this year, who I know has a crush on me. He probably doesn't think I know that he does, but it's obvious he does.

He walks with my friend Allie and me to Chorus every morning. He's one of the male singers in our class. He's kinda cute and is the only one with a mustache in the eighth grade. He looks more grown-up than the other boys in our school.

Donna M. Zadunajsky

Usually before classes, Allie, Tyler, who is my boyfriend, and Shawn hang out at my locker. I've noticed a tall skinny boy with dark brown hair walk by my locker and smile at me every day. Part of me wants to know his name, but I also don't want my boyfriend to think there's something going on between us, when in all honesty, I don't even know this kid's name or anything about him.

Then one day out of the blue, Shawn calls him over when he sees him walking down the hall towards us. "Hey, Mick. Come over here. I want to introduce you to my friends."

So, this Mick kid comes trotting over to my locker. He has a wide smile on his face, but at the same time, I can tell he's nervous about something. I honestly don't have a clue why he'd be nervous. There's no one in our small group that would treat anyone badly. We don't associate with kids like that.

Random Quote by Layla Manning:

When I first saw you, I was afraid to meet you. When I first met you, I was afraid to love you, but now that I love you, I'm afraid to lose you...

Friends

Weeks and months pass, and now we are like total best friends, Mick and me. He's so easy to talk too, and it's like he understands me, knows me. Unlike Tyler, who broke up with me because he likes someone else.

I don't even want to try to understand boys. First, they tell you they love you and next, they dump you for another girl. My mom says we're just too young for love. That we're thirteen; we don't even understand what love is. Maybe she's right.

*   *   *   *   *

I think my mom almost blew a gasket the other night with Bailey. We were at Sports Plex, which is a huge building of nothing but sports and fitness, playing basketball. Okay, I was playing basketball with my friends that are boys, and Bailey was sitting on the bleachers texting God knows who. Anyway, I find out that she called my mom telling her to ignore the texts that she would be getting from Allie, which I didn't find out until my mom called me and started asking me all these questions. She's pissed!

So here's the story:

Before Bailey and I went to the Sports Plex, she was on my iPad while I was finishing up my homework. My mom said all homework had to be done before we went, and it was a Friday. I told her that I had all weekend, but she wanted it done first.

So, okay, I finished my homework as Bailey was doing something on my iPad. Later, I find out that when Allie was over a couple of days before, she never logged out of her Snap/Chat account, and I guess Bailey thought it'd be funny to pretend she was Allie and have this conversation with Mick, saying she wanted to go out with him and do all this stuff with him.

So, when Bailey called my mom and told her to ignore the texts that Allie would be sending her, my mom got curious as to why Bailey would call and tell her that it was nothing. My mom did some investigating and was furious with Bailey and me, which I didn't even know Bailey had done. But, when my mom gets pissed, she's pissed!

My mom comes, picks us up, and has all of Baileys things in the backseat. She drops off *my want to be boyfriend* Jeff and then Bailey, without speaking one word to any of us. Once Bailey is dropped off, my mom tears into me about what happened. I explain to her that I had no idea what Bailey was doing. My mom said that I wouldn't be allowed at Bailey's house and that she would never come to our house ever again until I graduate and I was living in my own house.

My mom also said that she was and is a bad influence and that she doesn't want us hanging out outside of school. She said there was nothing she could do about us hanging out at school. So that's why Bailey and I are no longer friends.

<u>*Random Quote by Layla*</u>

<u>*Manning:*</u>

Your rude comments and insults only make me stronger than I really am...

Mick

Mick and I are on Kik, SnapChat, and we even Oovoo together. Sometimes, when we don't want to be bothered by our other friends—we FaceTime together.

I've noticed lately that Mick has been posting some sad quotes on his site. I'm not sure what to think of them, if I should even take them serious or not.

There's this one that's called *"I'm Sorry."* I think it's meant for me, but when I ask him about it, he avoids my question and changes the subject.

I've mentioned some of the things he does and says, to my mom. She just says to keep him on the phone and to continue to make sure he is okay. She also said, she wished this wasn't something I had to go through with a friend. She thinks he could be suicidal.

* * * * *

We had this fight the other day, Mick and I. Now, we're not talking, though it's more me than him. He doesn't like Bailey, and says I'm a different person when she's around. I don't see how? I'm me. Just like my mom said, she can't stop me from hanging out with Bailey at school.

I think I remember my mom saying something like that about me too. That when I'm talking to Mick, I'm a different person—I'm somewhat mean to others. Also, that I'm walking around like I'm 'Queen' of the house. She says, I should just be myself, and if people don't like me for who I am, then they're not worth my time or my friendship.

So now, we're not talking and it's my entire fault. I miss talking to him, with him. He's like my best friend in the whole world. I just don't understand why it feels like everyone is against me, since Bailey and I can't spend any more time together outside of school.

<u>*Random Quote by Layla*</u>

<u>*Manning:*</u>

I think I really need to think about you even more than I already do & figure out how much you actually mean to me, so I know how much I need you & how much you actually care about me & my choices...

Scars

Now, since the holiday vacation started, I've wanted more and more to call Mick and talk to him. It's not like I can't call him, it's just that I'm afraid he won't want to talk to me. Won't want to be my friend anymore.

I decide to call him anyway, that's really the only way I'll know if he'll pick up the phone, right? I scroll through my contacts and hover my finger over his name. Without thinking, I push the video icon and it starts to ring on his end.

Two, then three rings.

Maybe he doesn't want to talk to me, doesn't want to be my friend. Next thing I know, I see his face staring back at me.

"Hi," I say.

"Hi," he says back.

"How's your winter break going?" I ask.

"Good, I guess."

"Cool," I reply, and then all is quiet.

I can see part of his face and I wonder what he's thinking about. I wonder if it's me, he's thinking of. Maybe he misses me too.

He asks me what I've been doing since school has let out. "How's your break going?"

"It's alright, bored as all hell," I say.

"Ya', me too. My dad's at work, so I can't really go anywhere and it's too cold to hang outside. "

"That's sucks," I agree. "I'm just laying in bed, watching TV. I don't feel like doing much today."

We both get quiet. The next few words out of his mouth surprises me, "I wrote you a letter," he says.

"You wrote me a letter? When can I read it?" I reply, smiling.

"I guess when we go back to school," he says.

"That's like two weeks away! I can't wait that long!" I shriek. "Can't you bring it to my house?"

"I'll have to call my dad and ask. Will your mom be able to come and get me?"

"I'll ask my mom and then you can ask your dad."

"Ok," he replies.

I get out of bed and walk through my room. I mute my end so I can ask my mom if he can come over. Sometimes, if she has a lot to do with her writing, she tends to over react and gets upset.

She said "yes" that Mick can come over for a few hours, but that I have to find out if Allie can come over because the rules were "no boys over without another girl over". I guess I understand, but at the same time I think the rule sucks, and that it feels like my parents don't trust me with a boy, even though we are just friends, nothing more.

I walk back to my bedroom, as I'm texting Allie and asking if she can come over for a few hours and that we'd pick her up if she can. Only a few seconds pass when she replies that she can. "Cool," I text back, "Be there in about half an hour."

Minutes go by, before, I tell Mick that he can come over and that my mom will come and pick him up. I wait for him to let me know what his dad says. Mick texts back that he can come over but has to be home by eight. I hurry, get changed, and do my hair.

Forty-five minutes later, we are driving through Mick's community, looking for his home. My moms GPS says we are at our destination, but the numbers to the house don't match. I text Mick and ask him to come outside so we can see him.

Once he's in the car, he is quiet. My mom introduces herself and we are off driving towards home. He notices Allie, but doesn't say anything. I text him that I have to have a friend over, so I'm not alone with a boy, he texts back that it's okay.

We arrive at my house, I show Mick around, and then Allie, Mick, and I go downstairs to be away from my mom. She likes quiet when she writes.

We three are on our phones texting other friends. I know, I have friends over, but yet, we are all texting other friends. Can't explain it. My mom says that we kids don't know how to socialize, and that we would've never survived as kids in the eighties when she was in school. There were no cell phones. If you were bored, you found something to do, or her parents gave her something to do, which was work related. I don't do work, if I don't have too.

So we're all texting and I notice that Mick pushes the sleeves of his jacket up on both arms. I see several. No, more than several, scars, which look like cut marks.

He looks at me, but I quickly look down at my phone, pretending I didn't notice. I close my eyes, hoping that I was just seeing things, but when I look back up, his sleeves are back down, so that only tells me that it's true. I did see cut marks on both of his arms.

Before I know it, it's time to take him home. But before he gets out of the car, he slides the note he wrote me across the seat and gets out. We wait until he's in the house before driving off.

Random Quote by Layla Manning:

I don't want to lose you like I lose everybody else...

Letters

Later after dropping Allie off, I was sitting in my room reading the letter Mick wrote me.

Dear Layla,

We haven't talked for almost two months, tbh (to be honest) that was because you were hanging around Bailey, and I don't like her. I hate her and she makes you a different person. It wasn't for the better that you changed. Honestly, I didn't like you when you were around her. Now that you are not friends with her, you are back to your old self again, and I like that. You were my bestest friend ever and I trusted you with everything, lol. I

*still do, trust you. Well, almost
everything. I miss you and it sucks to
lose you tbh, but it's my entire fault
because I'm the one who made the
decision not to be friends. It was a huge
mistake, but that's not something I can
just take back so... even though we are
not friends I still love you with all my
heart; no matter what I'm always here
for you if you need to talk or vent. You
still mean the world to me and I will
still do anything for you. Just wanted to
say that I still love you. You are
amazing in every way and I miss
talking with you, and FaceTiming with
you. I hope that one day you will
realize how much you mean to me. I
mean it when I say, "I love you"—
unlike you, I actually love you. Whether
you know it or not, I really still like*

you, lol, (laugh out loud). You're the only person who knows who I really like, besides that person. Don't tell anyone!! I think Allie and me are friends, but idk (I don't know), tbh, idc (I don't care) if we are friends, but yeah, I just wanted you to know how much I miss hanging out with you and talking with you when we're not in school. Hope you write back to me. So, yeah, I guess this is goodbye.

-Mick

I wipe the tear from my cheek because in all honesty, I've really missed my friend too. I'm glad I reached out to him and we're talking again. I can't believe I let Bailey get between us like that. He's my best friend, and I care a lot about him.

I decide I'm going to write him back a letter as well. I climb off my bed and grab a handful of loose-leaf paper, sitting in a bin on my desk. I slide the tray from underneath my bed, climb back under the covers, and start writing.

I stop as a memory of his arms flash back into my mind. I never knew that Mick cut himself. He has never confided in me about things like that, and I wonder how I can be his best friend if he hides something as bad as cutting from me. He has never mentioned anything bad happening to him, not that something tragic had to have happened for him to make cuts on his arms. I guess; I'm just assuming, something bad occurred in his life. I wonder if I should ask him about it. If he'd actually be honest with me. Maybe that's something I should talk to my mom about and see what she says.

Dear Mick,

I really enjoyed reading your letter to me, and I have to tell you that I have missed you too. I'm glad I called you today, and you were able to come to my house. You're my best friend as well, and I'm glad we can go back to the way it was. I'm sorry for acting different when I was hanging around Bailey; idk that I was acting different. I guess you're not the only one who feels that way.

You didn't seem to like the fact that Allie was over, but yeah, sorry about that. Mom says, "Rules are rules." Whatever, I can't wait until I'm old enough to have my own place, and do whatever I want, when I want. I won't have to worry about having a boy over without another girl, lol.

You may not know this, but I do love you too. You are like my bestest friend in the world too, and I'm sorry for acting different. If I knew I was going to lose you over her, then I wouldn't have let her be my friend.

You know she can be persuasive sometimes and make people like her, but as you know, she is nothing but DRAMA...

Idk how I lost you to her, but I'm sorry. There I said it. I'm sorry for choosing her over you, when I know you are so much better than her. I seriously can go on and on about this, but I know you have better things to do than to read all of this.

I continued to write everything I felt down on paper, not stopping, even when my hand started to cramp up. It was past eleven when I decided to stop writing and end the letter, now six pages later. I think he will crap when he gets this.

Random Quote by Layla Manning:

Only focus on the things that make you happy, the other things cause you to just be very unfortunate...

Life

It's almost eight o'clock on a Friday night, and I decided to give Mick a call. I'm smiling at him, but I can't see his face because he has the camera facing the ceiling.

"Hi," I say.

"Hey," he replies.

"I read your letter and decided to write you one back, but I'll just give it to you on Monday when we go back to school," I state.

I think he's smiling, although he still doesn't let me see his face, but I can just tell that he's excited that I called him. Without realizing, Mick says "ouch" and my eyes widen a little. I try not to look afraid, knowing what he has just done to himself.

My mom comes into the room, and says "Hello" to Mick. "Hi, Mom," he says back to her. Most of the kids that I talk to call her mom or Mrs. Manning. My mom asks where Mick is because she can't see his face, then he makes his face visible. We talk for several more hours, until I start to fall asleep, and we're eventually disconnected.

* * * * *

Monday arrives and it's time to head back for the rest of the school year, now that the Christmas holiday is over. As usual, Shawn catches up to Allie and me as we head into the middle school for Chorus.

I can tell there's something going on with Shawn, but I'm having a hard time figuring it out. He's acting different around me. I get the feeling he still likes me, but I don't feel that way with him—about him. The worst part is, I'm not good at giving bad news. I don't do break-ups well. Let me rephrase that for you. Boys break up with me; I don't have the heart to break up with them. I can't stand the pain my heart feels when it's just not working out between us. Yeah, I'm only thirteen and have a lot to learn about love, so my mom says, but I know something because I feel sad when bad things happen.

* * * * *

My mom says I need to be stronger, grow stronger. Life isn't easy and sometimes when you're in a relationship that just isn't working, you have to let go and move on or you'll just grow up to be a bitter person. I think when she tells me that she's talking about my real dad. I don't know everything he did, but what she has told me is that he's an alcoholic and was very verbal abusive with her and physical at times. She had to finally take me out of the house because she wanted to give me a better life. She wrote a book about it, but says I can't read it yet because there are some inappropriate things written that I'm not old enough to read yet. Boy, if only she knew the things we kids talk about.

Like my adopted dad, for instance, he tends to swear a lot, but says that I probably hear worse things around my friends. Still, he shouldn't swear around me like that, besides my mom tells him all the time to stop because she heard it all the time from my real dad, and she doesn't need to hear it with him.

My parents don't really fight, but my mom has been standing up for me more lately. At first, I think she was afraid of my adopted father, but now she doesn't put up with his shit! Life's too short to be unhappy, to be stuck in a rut, as I call it.

Random Quote by Layla

Manning:

Everyone who says hello, will one day say goodbye; sometimes without a warning, or give a reason why...

Football Time

I can't believe how fast January came and went. We went back the first week of the new year and the teachers slammed us with homework. With all the work they've been giving us, I hadn't had much time to think about Mick. Yeah, we talk, but I'm talking about what he's possibly doing to himself. I wonder if he cuts himself every day. If he feels that he's not important to anyone or if he just wants to die.

I hope not because then I'd lose someone that I care a lot about. Someone that is my best friend in the whole world. But, what if he feels more for me than I feel for him. Does that mean I will be responsible for him taking his life, if he does? Will I be the one going to jail if just one time, he cuts too deep?

I honestly don't want to think about it. I don't want to feel or be responsible for what he may be doing to himself. Is that wrong of me? Should I be held accountable for his death, if it should happen?

I close my science book and toss it aside on the bed. I just have some math to finish, and then I will be done with all my homework for the weekend.

I look up and spot the huge monkey Mick has given me, sitting next to my television. Funny story actually. It's the beginning of February and Mick rides his bike over in forty-degree weather to my house with this gigantic monkey, sitting on the handlebars. He said it's my early Valentine's Day present, along with a box of chocolates. Wow, right!

* * * * *

Even though I don't plan to go anywhere this weekend, I might ask to have a friend over. The temperature outside today when I got home from school was nineteen degrees. I remember when I first came to Illinois, and the first snowfall came. It was awesome, although I was eight at the time, just five years ago, and now I don't like the cold one bit. Moving back to Florida would be a plus, but I don't want to leave all my friends behind.

* * * * *

It's Super bowl Sunday, and my parents are in the living room watching the game. My mom wants the New England Patriots to win, who are playing against the Seattle Seahawks.

She comes in during commercials to see what I'm up to. I've been sleeping in the back bedroom because my room is being repainted and they're putting in a wood floor. I can't wait to see it when it's done. I chose a teal color, darker on two walls, and lighter on the opposite ones. It's going to look awesome. I'm also getting a new bed. I want a white one with drawers on the end.

Everyone is hoping that it snows a foot outside so school will be canceled. An hour later, my mom comes in and says that the school called and there is no school tomorrow. What a coincidence. We were all thinking and wishing it to happen, and the next thing we know, it happens!

Another hour later, the game is over and my mom is cheering that New England won. She does this dance in my room as she watches the final touchdown being made by an interception. My friends are all laughing at her. They think she's so cool; she's okay sometimes, but only when I'm not being yelled at for bad grades or something stupid like that.

Tyler says goodbye and then Bailey, who no one really talked to the whole time she was on. Now it's just Shawn, Mick, and me left. We're all doing our own thing. I'm watching TV, Shawn has his earbuds in and doing something on his iPod or whatever he has in his hands. Mick, I'm not sure what he's doing. His iPod is on mute and facing the ceiling again. I'm a little afraid he might be cutting himself while he's Oovooing with us.

I look away and watch the show that's on the TV, and then back at my iPad. I blink because I'm not sure what I saw was real. Mostly, I don't want to believe what Mick just did. What Shawn and I both saw as we looked at our devices at the very same time. Mick must have seen it too, because once he pulled the gun out from his mouth, the screen went black.

<u>Random Quote by Lalya</u>

<u>Manning:</u>

I know sometimes I mess things up, and it seems like I don't care, but to be honest, you're my everything just because I let you go, doesn't mean

I wanted too...

Not Knowing

Sleep was something I didn't get much of last night. When my mom comes in to the back bedroom the following morning, I wasn't sure if I should say anything to her. She knows about the cuts he makes on his arms, but I'm not sure what this will do to her. Will she call the police and have them go to his house? I don't want to lose him. I don't want them to put him away in some crazy house. But mostly, I don't want him to be dead.

He's my best friend and I want him around for the rest of my life. How do I tell him, when he's not answering my calls—my texts? Maybe the best thing to do is to have my mom call the cops. This way I'll know for sure he's still alive.

"Mom," I say as I roll over to look at her face.

"Yes, Sweetie?" she replies.

I take in a deep breath, wanting to tell her never mind, but I can't. I need to tell her what I saw. What Mick had in his mouth last night before he disconnected. "There's something I want to talk to you about."

She takes a seat on the bed beside me. "Sure, what do you want to talk about?" She combs her fingers through my hair as she waits for me to speak.

"You remember me telling you about Mick and the cuts on his arm?"

She nods.

I swallow, and then continue. "Well last night I saw him..." I stop, wanting to take it all back. To have never said one word to her.

"What is it? Is everything okay with Mick?"

I shake my head, "I don't know."

She stares at me for a long time, waiting for me to continue, but I don't know if I can.

"Has something happened to him?" She looks nervous and a little scared. Her eyes are searching mine for an answer, but I don't think she will find one.

"Last night when I was on Oovoo with Mick and Shawn. I saw him... I saw him put a gun in his mouth and when he noticed his iPod was facing him, he disconnected and I haven't been able to get a hold of him since. He won't respond to my calls, Mom," I say in one long breath.

She sucks in a quick breath, and then stands. She starts to pace the room as if waiting for an answer. She stops and faces me, "I'm going to write an email to the guidance counselor at the school. If he should reply to you then we know he's alive, but I think it's time the school knows about this and that he finally gets the help he needs. Do you have his dad's phone number?"

"No," I reply.

"That's fine. That's okay," she says as if thinking she needs to reassure me and not herself, and then leaves the room.

I continue to text him and check my Snap/Chat, just in case he's on it and doesn't want to talk to me.

Nothing.

I roll over and throw the blanket over my head. I don't want to get out of bed, and I'm grateful that school is canceled for today.

As I start to doze off again, I feel my cell phone vibrate beside me under the covers. I glance at my phone to see who it is. It's not him so I flip it back over, closing my eyes. I hear my mom come into the room, but she must have seen that I was hiding under the blankets and leaves the room, closing the door behind her.

* * * * *

A couple of hours later and still no response from Mick, I contemplate what I should do today. I could stay under the covers, but I know my mom won't let that happen. She's one of those moms that stay busy all the time, not wanting to rest for one second. I think she thinks if she doesn't do it at this moment, it won't get done. Oh, and it needs to be done her way.

I throw back the covers and head into the bathroom, and then see what's in the kitchen for me to eat. I'm not big on breakfast so I grab a pop tart and go see what my mom is up to.

She's sitting at the computer, like that surprises me, writing an email. The printer starts printing and she tells me to grab it and read what it says:

Dear Cathy,

It has come to my attention that one of the students at Homer Jr. High is being bullied. I was also made aware that he, Mick Connors, has been cutting as well as posting suicidal posts on all of his social media accounts. My daughter has confided in me, and not knowing what else to do as I don't know his parent's phone numbers, I decided to inform the school about what has been happening with one of your students.

I have collected documents of things that he wrote and has done to himself. I can drop them off at the school if you need them. You can reach me at 885-555-2323 or by email if you have any further questions about what is going on.

Thank you,

Mrs. Manning

I nod and hand the paper to my mom, "What do you think they'll do to him?" I ask.

"I hope they get him the help he needs. There has to be a reason why he's doing this. Something had to have happened to him. Something he doesn't know how to cope with. I know you care, but honey, he needs help. I know you think you can help him, but he really needs to see someone who deals with this all the time," she says.

"I know Mom, but he tells me all the time that I'm a great friend and that he can't live without me, talking to each other helps," I plead.

"Honey," she replies as she smooths her hand down my arm and holds onto my fingers. "We... you, can't help everyone in the world. He's asking in his own way for help. He just doesn't know any other way to do it, and by us taking the first step and letting the school know about these kids bullying him and in return him cutting himself, I'm hoping it's not too late. That we didn't wait too long to get him help."

I nod, knowing she's right, but still deep inside I ask myself if I could've done something to help him, instead.

<u>Random Quote by Layla</u>

<u>Manning:</u>

Side by side or miles apart, we are best friends connected always by heart...

Tuesday

The next morning, my mom gets me up for school. I sit at the edge of my bed, trying to wake up, but my mind is still on Mick. He hasn't answered any of my texts or my calls all day yesterday. I want to go to school to see him; I'm hoping and praying to see him there. I don't think I can handle it *if* he isn't there. *If* he did what I saw him doing.

I stand outside waiting for the stupid bus to come; it's freaking cold outside. This would have to be the first time I actually want to go to school, or at least to the one place that'll ease my mind and either make it all better or make it worse.

Fifteen minutes later, I'm at the school, scoping the crowd of kids, anxious to see him, but I don't. I turn and catch up with Allie before I'm late for Chorus. Shawn's with us too. I want to ask him if he saw anything the other night, but I don't want to do it in front of Allie or the other kids. I don't want anyone but us to know what might have happened to Mick.

After Chorus, I'm called down to the office. Everyone is looking at me like I've done something wrong. I grab my things and head down the stairs to the front office. A woman named Cathy, meets me at the front desk, takes me to a small room, and closes the door. My heart is beating a mile a minute. Part of me feels like I'm going to throw-up everywhere.

Cathy sits down in front of me and slides a stack of papers towards me. I only have to see part of it to know what it is. My mom must've printed them out to show the school. You know, as proof that something is or was going on.

An image of Mick flashes in my mind. The one with a gun in his mouth. The last image I have of him. Cathy hasn't said anything on whether he's done it or not. Why won't she tell me?

"Layla," Cathy says, "Can you tell me who posted these?"

I swallow before answering, "Mick Connors."

"Has he ever talked to you about suicide?"

I shake my head.

"Can you tell me how you found out about the cuts on his arm?"

"I saw them for the first time when he came over to my house."

"And when was that?"

"Right after Christmas," I say. My palms are beginning to sweat and I wipe them on my jeans.

"Did he show them to you?"

"No." I shake my head, again. "He pushed the sleeves of his sweatshirt up, but when he saw that I had seen them, he quickly covered them up."

"Did you say anything to him?"

"No, I told my mom."

"And what did she say?"

"She told me to just keep him talking when we're on the phone and to make sure that if he's depressed about something to text with him and not to say anything that would push him away. Nothing that would make him not want to talk to me, and also that he may be suicidal."

"That's some good advice, but what made you finally want to come forward and let the school know?" she asks.

I take in a deep breath, still trying to calm down my stomach. "On Sunday after the football game. It was late, maybe one or two in the morning. He always has his iPod facing the ceiling, but sometimes I can see his face. This time, I saw the ceiling, but when I looked at my TV and then back at the screen, it was on him and he...he had a gun in his mouth," I replied, feeling as if I had said too much. I didn't want him to get into trouble, but mostly, I worried that he had actually done it. Cathy hasn't told me he has or hasn't—yet.

"Thank you, Layla. For right now, you can go to your next class, and I will call you back to the office a little later. I don't want you to talk to anyone about this. What is said here stays here. Are you okay with that?"

I nod and quickly stand and grab my books. Once, I get my hall pass, I walk to my locker and exchange textbooks. An hour passes since I'd been in the office and now I'm on my way to English.

The one thing that sucks the most is that Mick and I don't have one single class together. The only time we see one another is when we pass in the hallway. I'm hoping that will be after this class.

* * * * *

No sooner, than I enter the class, it's over and I'm leaving and heading back to my locker. As I place my books inside, I feel a tap on my shoulder. I quickly turn around, but it's Shawn, not Mick.

"Hey, how come you were in the office so long last period?" Shawn asks.

As I was told not to say anything, I hadn't come up with a false excuse to replace the real one. But thank goodness for my quick thinking, I reply, "My mom was talking to one of my teachers and they wanted to discuss it with me," I shrug, hoping he doesn't ask any more questions. Although I still want to know if he saw what I had, Shawn doesn't seem different than any other time we've talked. So, I decide to let it go and not think about it as much.

I turn and grab what I need and close my locker. I still haven't seen Mick, which was really starting to make me worry. Shawn and I walk to our next class together, but neither of us says a word.

Five minutes after we get to class, Mick's name in announced over the loud speaker, and my stomach drops. I knew it didn't mean he was here, but it also didn't mean he wasn't.

The rest of day crawls by, and in my last class, my teacher answers the phone on her desk, and then tells me that I'm needed in the office again. I grab my things and head out the door, not once looking at the kids in the class.

This time when I'm in the office, Vice Principal Stevenski is talking to me and asking me pretty much the same questions as before. Still no word on whether Mick is here or not.

Next thing I know, my mom is entering the room with Cathy. She looks at me, and then at Vice Principal Stevenski before taking a seat. He went over what he talked to me about and asks if there's anything else we need to add to our story. He makes it seem like we're the bad guys. *They wouldn't have known if it weren't for us,* I think to myself.

Not soon after my mom arrives that we are on our way home. She's in the kitchen going through the mail when I come to her with my cell phone. There's someone calling with a number I don't know.

"Can you answer it?" I ask. "I don't know who it is."

She takes the phone from me and says "Hello", then mouths to me that it's Mick's dad. He wants to know where Mick is because he never texted him when he got home from school. She tells him she doesn't know, but then turns to me and whispers that she needs to tell him what happened today that he should know. That she would want to know if it were the other way around.

She heads into the office off the living room and sits down. I follow listening to every word she says to Mick's dad. It had to be twenty minutes later, when she hangs up with him and tells me what was said.

"Mick's dad didn't know about Mick cutting himself. He didn't know that he was being bullied at school, either. Right before we hung up, the school was calling him so he said he'd talk to me later and let me know what was happening." I nod, and then she tells me to start on my homework, while she cooks dinner.

* * * * *

Finally by eight that night, Mick's dad texts my mom and says that Mick is okay, and that they were at the hospital getting him evaluated.

I exhale the breath I was holding. Mick was going to be okay. He was going to get help. My phone vibrates, I look down and it's him, it's Mick. I feel nervous at first wondering if he is mad at me for saying something. If we'll remain friends after what I said—what I did. That, I didn't know. I had to leave that up to him to decide. If I could choose just one prayer out of the many that I've made in my lifetime, it would be that we stay together—friends, or something much more, but it's not my decision to make.

Random Quote by Layla Manning:

*Before you leave me again, tell me, so I can let you know if I'm ready to watch you go...

*It's going to be hard to stay away from someone who means so much to me...

*Until you came along, I never knew how much I'd be missing...

Epilogue
6 Months Later...

That night six months ago, it had to be my friend Ray, who made the gun jam and not work. Not that I don't believe in God, but I do believe that my best friend was watching me from somewhere and at that moment in time, he had stopped me from killing myself. The same way he had ended his life. There was no other way to explain it. When the trigger didn't click and I couldn't get the cylinder open, I knew it had to have been something or someone. I could see into the barrel and noticed the bullet in the slot ready to fire.

The one bullet that would have ended my life.

Ended everything that I cared so much about.

You're all probably wondering what happened to Layla and me? Did I forgive her and if we remained friends? Did I still want to end my life? Do I still cut my arms and legs? Do I still blame myself for my best friend killing himself?

Yes, I can say that I do still blame myself a little for Ray dying. I should've known and done something to help him. He had always been there for me. I in-turn walked away, thinking he was just messing around with his dad's gun. That he wouldn't do anything stupid—like kill himself.

Ray wasn't stupid, but what he was, was being bullied. Bullied to the point where he didn't want to live anymore. So what if he was different? So what if he was attracted to other boys? Being gay shouldn't have given those other boys a reason to belittle him or to do horrific homophobic things to him—at him.

There were times when he couldn't walk down the hall without someone laughing at him and teasing him. The other kids would make comments about us being a couple, which we weren't. They just wouldn't stop. Wouldn't leave him alone. And I believe they're happy he's dead, and nothing bad will ever happen to them for doing what they did to him. Justice wasn't served!

I liked Ray. No, I loved him, and he was my best friend in the world. He was the nicest kid I had ever met, and he'd do anything for anyone.

Me? I couldn't handle life without him beside me. Until I met Layla Manning.

No, I don't cut anymore, no matter what life throws my way. I can't say I don't miss it because to me, it released something inside me that I can't explain. Something that helped me to get up in the morning and take my first step. Cutting was something that helped me live one more day and put up with the kids that bullied me.

With therapy, I don't want to end my life. In all honesty, I only wanted the evil thoughts to go away. I wanted the pain to end. I wanted to be released from the guilt of not saving my best friend. Although I know I can't bring him back, I also know that it isn't or wasn't my fault what happened.

Even though I'd left my old school and no one at Homer knew me, there were other bullies. Kids that didn't know about me or what had happened to Ray. They still found something about me they didn't like. I walked funny, or I was too skinny and looked like a skeleton. Though at my other school, I was considered overweight. I was just someone who didn't stop them from being mean to me.

No matter where you go, what you wear, or who you hang out with, there will always be people finding fault and bullying you about it. But, I think someone else bullies the people who bully other kids. Either from someone they live with, or maybe they just hold some kind of hatred inside themselves and they feel they need to express it by doing it to someone else.

I don't know because that's not who I am. I don't get off on hurting other kids, other people. I, like everyone else, just want to be liked. We all want and need friends to breathe. It's who we are.

As for Layla, I have forgiven her for telling her mom and for Mrs. Manning for telling the school what I was doing and about to do. Layla and I are not only best friends, but also she and I have a relationship that I couldn't imagine having with another girl. She is my girlfriend, and we have been together for the past four months. We talk all the time, and I let her know when I'm having a bad day.

The therapist I see tells me it's good to have an open relationship and that if things don't last with Layla, I will be okay. I will still live on another day, and my heart will heal. I will always meet someone else, but for now, my therapist says to be happy and enjoy every day that I have left. No matter what obstacles I may run into, I'll just need to take it one day at a time.

Kids like my best friend Ray, he had another choice to make, but decided to choose the one he couldn't take back. He couldn't un-pull the trigger, but he could've told his parents and gotten help, and then the school would've known what was happening and he'd still be here right now. As much as I would like to go back in time, I can't. I can't bring him back, and even if I'd stopped him that night, would he have tried again?

No one knows what someone might do. But if you do know someone who needs help, or someone you think is depressed, there's never a wrong choice. Tell a parent or another adult. Let them know that you or someone you know needs help and may be suicidal.

I hope that my story helps people like me and that you know you're not alone. There are others out there just like us—going through something, we don't understand. There is help, and people to talk to.

HELP ME!

People that cut are not trying to kill themselves. They are just trying to relieve the pain they have and feel inside. They just want whatever happened to disappear and by cutting, it's our way of breathing one more day. We're no different than anyone else. We just can't handle things like others can. There are things out there that are scary. Things that are done to others, done to us; things we didn't ask for or wish upon. So, cutting is what helps us to get by. To breathe another day. I don't think anyone really wants to die. I just think; we think; there's just no other way out. No other way to relieve the pain trapped inside us...

No matter what kind of challenges or difficulties or painful situations you go through in your life, we all have something deep within us that we can reach down and find the inner strength to get through them.

—Alana Stewart

More books by Donna M. Zadunajsky

Children's Books

Tayla's Best day Ever!

Tayla's Best Friend

Tayla's New Friend

Tayla goes to Grammie's House

Tayla Takes a Trip

Tayla's Day at the Beach

Tayla's First Day of School

Novels:

Broken Promises

Not Forgotten

Family Secrets *"Secrets and Second Chances," Book 1*

Hidden Secrets *"Secrets and Second Chances," Book 2*

About the Author

Donna M. Zadunajsky started out writing children's books before she accomplished and published her first novel, *Broken Promises*, in June 2012. She then has written several more novels and her first novella, *HELP ME!*, which is a subject about suicide and bullying.

Her third novel *Family Secrets, "Secrets and Second Chances"*, which is first in a series she is writing, was given a publishing contract through California Times Publishing.

You can follow me on Twitter, Facebook, Author website, and my blog.